Lucky Gemstone an

Talismanic

Charms

&

Amulets

For
Health, Wealth & Happiness

Robert W Wood D.Hp
(Diploma in Hypnotherapy)

Rosewood Publishing

First published in U.K. 2002
By Rosewood Publishing
P.O. Box 219, Huddersfield,
West Yorkshire HD2 2YT

www.rosewood-gifts.co.uk

Robert W Wood D.Hp
Asserts the moral right to be identified
As the author of this work

Copy-editing
Margaret Wakefield BA (Hons) London
www.euroreportage.co.uk

Cover photograph by
Andrew Caveney BA (Hons)
www.andrewcaveneyphotography.co.uk

Cover and layout re-designed by
AJ Typesetting
www.ajtype.co.uk

Printed in Great Britain by
Delta Design & Print Ltd
www.deltaleeds.co.uk

ISBN 978-0-9532930-8-7

TALISMANS, CHARMS AND AMULETS

**In our world of scientific achievements,
with its computers, aeroplanes, rockets, space travel
and the Internet, isn't it surprising to find that there still
remains an ancient 'magical-like' knowledge that
retains its grip on the human imagination.
And it's found in the form of lucky
Talismans, Charms and Amulets.**

Talismans.

A talisman is often a stone or other small object, sometimes inscribed or carved on, and believed to protect the wearer from evil influences, bad luck, mischief or ill health. The word 'talisman' comes from the Greek word 'telesma' meaning 'to consecrate or magically charge'. Throughout history, magical talismans have been used to help bring protection, power and prosperity to their wearer or owner. They are specifically designed to achieve a particular purpose, and are said to work by generating a positive energy that can help to achieve this.

Amulets.

Unlike talismans that need to be 'charged', amulets come already imbued with their own built-in power for health, wealth, energy, good luck and so on. There is a certain passiveness associated with the powers of an amulet. The possessor only needs to 'connect' by carrying, wearing or being near to it. The word 'amulet' is probably derived from the Latin 'amuletum', and may also have come from an Arab term 'hamala', which means 'to carry'.

Charms.

A charm is often a small object, a trinket, a piece of jewellery, and is often worn on a bracelet - a 'charm bracelet' - to protect, influence or heal, to attract good luck etc; a 'lucky charm'. The name is connected to the uttering of magical chants, a condition of 'enchantment'. The word 'charm' comes from the Latin word 'carmen' meaning 'a song'.

Using a kind of magic, a talisman can be endowed with a kind of supernatural power. This can be done either by using the forces of nature (for example, putting the talisman into a stream), or by a divine power (saying prayers), or by a ritualistic ceremony; or even by a combination of all three, depending on who's doing the 'charging'.

The word 'magic' can be used in many different ways. I use the word often in the sense that a spectacular fireworks display could be described as 'magical'. We live on a 'magical' planet; who could fail to be impressed by the splendour of a clear night sky, a sunrise or sunset, an electrical storm, a snowflake, spring flowers or autumn leaves? Or we can use the word 'magic' to mean any mysterious or extraordinary quality or power; you, the reader, will have to decide what is meant when you read 'magic' or 'magical'.

Throughout the ages.
A talisman can be any object that's believed to be endowed with magical powers. The item is active when it bestows this magical power upon the one who possesses it. Remember the story of Jack and the Beanstalk; it was the beans that were magical - they had been supercharged to grow into something very special: a giant beanstalk.

The Egyptians and Babylonians used talismans when attempting to alter the forces of nature. In the Middle Ages, holy relics and other objects assumed the value of talismans in attempts to cure illnesses.

There is a long tradition throughout history of talismans being made by alchemists, shamans, witches and priests. Alchemical charms were often worn by Kings and Queens, diplomats and merchants, popes and bishops. Less expensive amulets, usually made by witches, were worn or hung in the house by nearly everybody else. The most common amulets were those that protected against violence, plague, theft and bad luck.

Many alchemists sought the assistance of talismans, which they made in elaborate ceremonies. These were conducted during periods of auspicious astrological occasions, an example being during a full moon. Whilst performing these rituals they would recite incantations to conjure up the desired spirits, the ones who would imbue the talisman with magical power.

A talisman most sought after would have been the 'Philosopher's Stone', which many alchemists thought would transform base metals into silver or gold, therefore transforming, at the same time, their own fortunes.

J. K. Rowling, author of the book 'Harry Potter and the Philosopher's Stone', which has also been made into a film, changed it and decided that the Philosopher's Stone, for her, would be the 'Elixir of Life'.

Some legendary lucky talismans.

Who could forget that the sword 'Excalibur' gave King Arthur magical powers? Followers of St. Patrick, the patron saint of Ireland, have adopted the Shamrock as a symbol of luck - 'the luck of the Irish'. During the time of the Crusades, Nordic countries employed their special magical alphabet known as the 'Runes' for protection.

Legend has it that the undead (vampires) cannot attack if you hold up a cross - the symbol of God - as good deflects evil. Although crosses are not employed as a deflector of vampires today, at most Catholic funerals many attendees have crucifixes around their necks, although they probably don't usually wear them as everyday jewellery. The Christian fish, an ancient sign of Christ, is often seen on the backs of cars as an amulet, signifying that the owner wishes to be protected from evil. The scarab, the sacred beetle of ancient Egypt, is thought to possess the power to control the Sun and Immortality.

The lists goes on and on. Here are a few more: a horseshoe, a corn dolly, a dream-catcher, the seal of Solomon, the Kara, the ankh, a Buddha, the crescent, a St. Christopher, a lucky elephant, owl, cat or frog, a four-leafed clover, a wishbone, a wheel and so many more, depending on your culture.

Just like amulets, talismans play a significant part in everyday life. For example, in most religious traditions sacred books like the Torah, the Bible and the Koran are believed by some to possess special protective powers. This power is even carried over into the law courts of the world, where we swear to tell the truth by placing our hand on a holy book.

Modern talismans

Think of a rosary. Although the precise number of beads may vary from religion to religion, the purpose remains the same: to keep count of the number of devotional prayers being recited. But some believe they also have special protective powers.

New knowledge.

Although science has now an explanation for many of the phenomena that once baffled us, it is still a long way from being able to explain all of the mysteries that surround life. This is often left to others, and this is where religion or philosophy seems to step in and try to help. In ancient times it would have been alchemists, shamans, witches and priests. A few decades ago, computers, telephones, rockets, planes and satellites would have been objects described by everyone as being 'magical' or fanciful.

New knowledge seems to be arriving on a daily basis and at breakneck, phenomenal speed. Have you noticed how time seems to be speeding up? We have now truly entered into a new world, and this world is based on an incredible amount of knowledge.

It now begs the question: can talismans, charms and amulets have a place in this new world?

You may be surprised, but I think the answer is still 'yes', because I believe they fulfil an important role. They form a bridge from the past to the future, because they still can excite the imagination. Understand: I don't think they are a substitute for our natural instincts or built-in 'inner powers' or wisdom; but they can be a useful tool to help us see and then use the 'universal life force' that is inherent throughout the whole of the universe and in the forces of nature.

With the help of our minds, and especially our imaginations, and by employing our knowledge, we can begin to use this 'magic' to enrich both our own and others' lives. We are beginning to see that nature, the 'universal life force', mysteriously is interlinked with our bodies, minds and spirits.

Discovering a greater meaning.

The function of a talisman is to help make things possible; to bring about powerful transformations; to help a person who would not feel confident within themselves without a little help. A talisman can initially be that help. It's a useful tool. It's a little like phoning a helpline - you have a problem and you need help - except there's no-one there to take your call, only an answering machine. So you leave a message and hope someone will listen and then get back to you with help later. In this analogy the phone represents the talisman; it's the tool, it's a way of connecting.

Our journey through life is all about personal empowerment and freedom of choice, and what we do with it. Some people seem to be able to manifest their own power quite naturally, whilst others struggle to get past anything that controls their 'free will'. And so throughout the history of humanity, people have placed their hope in inanimate objects, in the belief of gaining that extra little help.

Be lucky.

Whether you are a believer in the supernatural or not, to have a sense of control over the uncontrollable is one explanation for why many seem to believe in lucky talismans. This belief crosses all nationalities, intelligence, education and status.

I remember reading about a chairman of an amazingly successful company which was growing at a very rapid rate. A reporter who asked him if he could explain the reason behind his company's rapid growth may have been forgiven for being a little surprised at the answer: the chairman quite flippantly explained it was all down to his magic lucky beans, and then showed him some he had on his desk in the form of sweets.

Don't we all, in one way or another, practise rituals to attract good luck? Take a bride, for example: to attract good luck she will wear something old, something new, something borrowed and something blue. On the first day of each new month some people will say 'rabbits, rabbits' for good luck. How many people won't walk under ladders, or, if they spill salt, throw some over their left shoulder so as to avoid attracting bad luck. Some will turn over their money in their pockets at the sight of a new moon in the hope of attracting more. How about: 'If you see a penny, pick it up, and all the day you'll have good luck'.

Luck may be an illusion of control, but control is what we seek in a random world. Although it may have no basis in science, it certainly can affect how we feel. Talismans, lucky charms and amulets can give a sense of preparedness, a feeling of control and a more positive outlook on life, which in itself may give us that edge to help improve our lives for the better. We all need something to believe in, be it a faith, a lucky mascot, a talisman or a philosophy. You may be surprised to find what even Prime Ministers' wives believe in.

The Bioelectrical Shield.

In 1998 the British Prime Minister's wife, Cherie Blair, was seen wearing a 'stress-busting' metal-encased crystal talisman, a pendant said to contain a 'magical' configuration of quartz and other crystals which help to deflect away from the wearer negative electromagnetic radiation, the kind that's emitted from modern office equipment such as computers and mobile phones.

Designed by a chiropractor called Dr. Charles Brown in the early 1990s, the shield has proved immensely popular despite its high selling price. The formula for the pendant and the crystal configuration came to the doctor in a series of visions, when he heard voices telling him what to do.

Cherie Blair was reported to have said, after she had misplaced her shield once, how she had become distressed because, as she explained it, 'It keeps away the bad vibrations from my computer.' This must be the very latest, certainly the most modern of all talismans. Since time began men or women have found comfort in the belief that they are not alone; that there's more to life than meets the eye. This is what all the great religions, philosophers, teachers, mystics, holy men, sages and priests have all been saying; maybe one day, somehow, we will discover they were all telling the truth.

George Frederick Kunz (1856-1932).

Some of the oldest ever recorded talismans appear in a brilliant book called 'The Magic of Jewels & Charms', written by George Frederick Kunz in 1915. He was a distinguished self-taught mineralogist who, for more than half a century, was the gem expert for Tiffany & Co. New York. Here are a few extracts taken from his original book of 1915.

... among the many stones endowed by medieval belief with wonderful powers, may be reckoned the 'rainmaking stones'. The miraculous effect was produced by rubbing them against each other ...

... Oriental rain-stones noted by ... writers of medieval times ... rock crystal as a rain-compeller finds honour among the wizards of the Ta-Ta-Thi tribe in New South Wales, Australia ...

... A mysterious stone mentioned three times in the Old Testament, each signifies a material noted for its hardness and translated 'diamond'; however, as it is almost certain that the Hebrews were not familiar with the 'diamond' it was most probably a variety of corundum ...

... fabled gem-bearing dragons of India were said to have sometimes fallen victims to the enchanter's art ...

... a stone described by Thomas de Cantimpre ... taken from the heart of a man poisoned, and kept for nine years, it gave protection from lightning, sudden death ...

... St. Hildegard of Bingen (1098 - 1179) wrote that 'just as a poisonous herb placed on a man's skin will produce ulceration'; by an analogous though contrary effect certain precious stones will, if placed on the skin, confer health and sanity by their virtue ...

How did she know? She heard voices telling her, in visions. She was one of the outstanding females of the 12th century and probably of the entire Middle Ages. She was a painter, composer, poet, scientist, playwright, prophet, preacher, abbess - and healer. From the time she was a young girl, Hildegard experienced visions. She claimed that angels described to her the healing properties of at least 25 stones.

... for centuries or more countless thousands, feeling assured of spiritual immortality, were nonetheless eager to have eternal youth and vigour and the power to peer into the future ...

Alchemists

... desire to find something by means of which gold could be made out of base metals; for youth and vigour, if coupled with poverty, are only half blessings. The search for the 'philosopher's stone' ... aimless pursuits of this end .. helped to lay the foundation of our modern chemistry...

... whether the conscious aim of the alchemist was the discovery of an actual stone, or merely the discovery of some process for turning a valueless substance into one of great value, is not clearly ascertainable from the purposely vague and obscure treatise on alchemy (Kunz is referring here to Ponce de Leon's 'Quest for the Foundation of Youth')

... the Alchemists believed that several other stones possessing 'magical' virtues could be produced. Among them: the Angelic stone, which gave power to see the angels in dreams and visions, and also the 'mineral stone', a substance by means of which common flints could be transmuted into diamonds, rubies, sapphires, emeralds etc. Possibly some alchemists were glassmakers and fused the quartz with various mineral salts into an imitation of the gems, therefore having the colours but not the hardness or other properties.

Stones.

... in British New Guinea - a native, who was suffering from Lumbago, fully believed the tale that his disease was caused by a stone embedded in his flesh. When the 'sorcerer' made passes over this man's back and pretended to remove a stone, the sufferer was convinced that the disease had left his body and he began to feel relief ...

...the burying of white stones or lumps of quartz with the dead was not infrequent in early times, in Ireland ... symbolic meaning of the colour of purity, white marble seems appropriate and beautiful for monuments ....

. St. Columba went to the river Ness and picked up out of its shallows several white pebbles - announcing that they would, by the Lord's power, work the cure of 'heathen' people. One of the stones was blessed by the saint and placed in a vessel filled with water; having taken a drink, the liquid restored his health ...

... a famous Scotch amulet - white quartz owned by the chiefs of Clan Donnachaidh and known as the 'stone of the Banner' ... was looked upon when first found as a powerful talisman in battle. And water in which it had been dipped was said to cure disease...

... the influence exercised by the text in Revelation (2.17): 'to him that overcometh ... I will give a white stone, and in the stone a new name written, which no man knoweth save he that receiveth it'.

... collections of stones and pebbles, often of little or no intrinsic value but supposed to possess occult powers, are handed down from father to son in many Hindu families of the poorer class ...

Amber.

... in ancient and medieval times the fear of poison being administered in food or drink was very great; and any substance that was credited with the power to show the presence of poison, by some change in clearness or colour, was highly valued. An Amber cup was said to reveal various kinds of poison ...

... the electrical property of amber was remarked as early as 600 B.C. by the Ionic philosopher Thales, and from this observation may be dated the beginning of the study of electrical phenomena ...

Romans used to hold balls of amber in their hands to keep cool ... the Chinese place pieces of amber on or in their pillows ... as proof of the extravagant value set upon amber by the Romans, sold at a higher figure than did a healthy, vigorous slave ...

Loadstone.
...in the seventeenth century a rupture, it was reported, was cured in 8 days by loadstone. The patient was first given a dose of iron filings, reduced to a very fine powder. A plaster made from crushed loadstone was applied externally to the affected part...

... in Medieval Europe, this mineral (loadstone) was greatly valued for its therapeutic virtues. Trotula, the first of the female physicians connected with the celebrated school of Salerno, the centre of medical culture in Europe in the Middle Ages ... recommended the use of loadstone in childbirth. The stone was to be held in the right hand ...

... That wounds caused by burning could be healed if powdered loadstone were sprinkled over them, was confidently taught even in the seventeenth century ...

A magnetised piece of steel looks exactly the same as an ordinary piece of steel - but the magnetised one can lift over twelve times its own weight, whereas the ordinary steel could not even lift a feather.

Magical protection.
There's always been a fascinating history or a symbolic background to talismans, charms and amulets. Even people who do not subscribe to the idea of magical protection will usually have some little object that they keep about them 'just for luck'; a little something just to help when facing the hazards of daily life.

Among these talismans and amulets are often found precious and semi-precious gemstones and crystals, each one possessing its own 'magical', historical and evolutionary curative power, a gift from nature; but can any be more beautiful than 'Birthstones' - steeped in history, born at the very beginning of the birth of our knowledge.

Birthstones.

Birthstones are used as lucky talismans to help bring good luck, health, wealth and happiness, and are often given to a newborn child. I have realised, mainly because of the many talks I have given over the years on 'the mysteries that surround gemstones and crystals', that most people seem to 'know' which their birthstone is; for example, it may be a diamond or a sapphire, an emerald or a ruby, a garnet or an opal, an amethyst or a pearl, etc, etc. They think, therefore, that the following list must be wrong. However, I discovered there are many lists. My list, printed below, contains only semi-precious gemstones. (To learn how I acquired this list, you'll find out more in my book 'Discover Why Crystal Healing Works'; details from the publishers - their address is given on the last page.)

However, I would like you to think about this: a diamond could not have been one of the original birthstones, because astrology dates back easily over six thousand years and no-one knew how to cut a diamond then. The art of cutting a diamond was only discovered a few hundred years ago, mainly because it takes a diamond to cut a diamond. So the diamond could not have been among the birthstones at that time. It now seems probable that what people mistook for a diamond was more likely to have been rock crystal.

After thorough and exhaustive research, I believe I have been able to establish as near genuine a list of birthstones as it is possible to get. My research was helped a lot, surprisingly, from the Scriptures, where there are two lists of twelve stones, one in the New and one in the Old Testament.

Sign	Dates		Birthstone
Aries	21st Mar	- 20th April	Red Jasper
Taurus	21st April	- 21st May	Rose Quartz
Gemini	22nd May	- 21st June	Black Onyx
Cancer	22nd June	- 22nd July	Mother of Pearl
Leo	23rd July	- 23rd Aug	Tiger Eye
Virgo	24th Aug	- 22nd Sept	Carnelian
Libra	23rd Sept	- 23rd Oct	Green Aventurine
Scorpio	24th Oct	- 22nd Nov	Rhodonite
Sagittarius	23rd Nov	- 21st Dec	Sodalite
Capricorn	22nd Dec	- 20th Jan.	Obsidian Snowflake
Aquarius	21st Jan	- 19th Feb	Blue Agate
Pisces	20th Feb	- 20th Mar	Amethyst

Theme stones.

The following lucky talismans and amulets are a list of stones taken from our range that's collectively been called 'Theme Stones. It's a range of the unusual and the humorous. There's a 'theme' behind each one, and although seemingly humorous at times, nevertheless they have been extensively researched to help find the right Gemstone or Crystal to create the ideal match for the following list of popular titles.

A Lucky *'Bingo Stone'*   **Obsidian Snowflake**
Carry this Gemstone with you and it may well be the way to your 'Jackpot'.

A *'Good Luck Stone'*   **Indian - Moonstone**
Allow this special Lucky Gemstone to help you attract your heart's desires.

'Lose a Stone' (for the weight watcher)   **Black Onyx**
Let this stone be your constant reminder to resist temptation.

'Love Stones'   **Amethyst**
Recognised as the Gemstone of true love, romance and faithfulness.

A *'Lucky Lottery Stone'*   **Green Aventurine**
Let the magical powers of this Gemstone help pick your winning numbers.

'Memory Stone' (to remember all)   **Rhodonite**
Memory going? Keep forgetting things? Then try this amazing Gemstone.

Achieve with a *'Milestone'*   **Red Jasper**
Aim for the top - set your targets and use this stone to achieve.

'Tranquillity Stone' for relaxing   **Rock Crystal**
Find your inner peace and calmness. and relax away your worries.

Use a *'Worry Stone'* to forget   **Tiger Eye**
Forget your problems. ease your mind. lift your spirits. and feel free.

For passion, an *'Adults Only Stone'*   **Carnelian**
A sensuous. imaginative aphrodisiac for those special 'adult' occasions.
    (There should be a health warning with this stone, Wow!)

Please Note

Any information given in this book is not intended to be taken as a replacement for medical advice. Any person with a condition requiring medical attention should consult a qualified doctor or therapist. **On no account should a gemstone or crystal ever be swallowed.**

Power Gems.

Gemstones and crystals are used as lucky talismans and amulets. There are times when they are better known for their healing powers. I have been extensively researching the healing nature of stones for many years. I have looked at many different sources for my information, including the Scriptures, always trying to discover the true identity of the most powerful and popular healing stones. Many are renowned for their mysterious, often 'magical-like' hidden powers. For thousands of years, ancient civilisations have been using these stones to help heal the mind. body and spirit. They were used to help attract to their owners their share of good luck. health. wealth and energy.

Although stones and crystals are very much a part of nature, these lovely, shiny. colourful stones and crystals are likened to a 'magnetic field'. They influence those coming into contact with them. You cannot see microwaves or radio waves but you know they exist. Each crystal, having its own unique 'signature' in the form of its 'energy frequency' , allows us to tune into that same frequency like changing the station on a television set. In this case you tune in to the 'healing' channel.

A Guide to the Power Within.

The following unique groups of Gemstones and Crystals are designed to carefully link in harmony and unite their individual mystic powers to provide a holistic 'force of energy', which can help revive health, increase wealth, bring peace and provide energy and vitality.

Healer.

Here are the three most powerful healing gemstones and crystals found during our research..............**Carnelian, Red Jasper and Rock Crystal.**

Good Luck.

The luckiest three Gemstones, all having a strong history with being lucky...........**Obsidian Snowflake, Green Aventurine and Moonstone.**

Peace of Mind.

A combination of stones to help bring peace, harmony and tranquillity into our surroundings ....**Green Aventurine, Rose Quartz and Rhodonite.**

For Willpower.
Stones and crystals that help to boost willpower, for losing weight or stopping smoking............**Rose Quartz, Black Onyx and Rock Crystal.**
Adults Only.
Combining stones to create the most imaginative aphrodisiac; a very sensuous combination.............**Amethyst, Rose Quartz and Carnelian.**
To Remove Aches and Pains.
When combined together, this combination can work wonders on aches and pains ....**Hematite, Rock Crystal and Rose Quartz.**
To Lift Depression.
A combination of stones that can help bring back joy and happiness whilst removing sadness...............**Carnelian, Tiger Eye and Hematite.**
The Elixir of Life.
To produce this: wash the stones, place in a glass of water, leave overnight, and sip slowly. Produces youthfulness...............**Rhodonite and Sodalite.**
Energy Booster.
Designed to help with tiredness; helps to see and feel 'life' with more energy, vigour and vitality........**Carnelian, Amethyst and Rock Crystal.**
Imagine.
Designed for a very special purpose, this helps to reach a level 'within the mind' for change ..**Green Aventurine, Amethyst and Rose Quartz.**
Fertility.
Crystal power designed to increase fertility, for that extra little help just when it's needed ....**Rock Crystal, Rose Quartz and Moonstone.**
Wisdom.
Gain the ability to think and act wisely using knowledge, insight, understanding and experience..........**Amethyst, Rose Quartz & Rock Crystal.**

The Modus Operandi.

Whether you can believe in these mystical powers or not, why not try focusing on your gemstones by holding them, and then at the same time imagine and concentrate on your desire, your dream, your ultimate goal. See it achieved within your mind's eye; believe there is someone or something listening, and that, just like a 'helpline' with an answering machine, they will respond as soon as they can, and help you in ways you probably couldn't even imagine. Allow your gemstone-crystals to act like a catalyst or sub-station to help boost your natural energy - an energy found within the human experience, within the mind.

"Is it the willpower to achieve that enables us to succeed?"

How to produce a lucky talisman.

You don't need to know how a telephone works to make a phone call - only how to speak!

To make a talisman, there must be a link, a bridge, to join with the 'universal life force' and the recipient. The talisman here is like the phone: acting as a catalyst, helping to bring these two things together. The more symbolic the ritual. the more it will bring about a connection.

A white cloth (handkerchief), a glass of water, a few grains of common rock or sea salt, a white candle and an incense stick are all you need to produce the most powerful, supercharged talisman.

Lay out the white cloth, then light the candle and incense stick. Clear your mind. Relax. Start thinking what you would like your talisman to achieve. Then imagine the desired end result; actually see it in your mind's eye. Believe, expect and let your subconscious - now helped by your imagination, in the form of your talisman - bring it to fruition.

Start this symbolic ritual. with expectancy. Although the 'universal life force' is invisible, nevertheless it is very real, and you are about to ask for its help. You are a child of the Universe; claim your inheritance.

The ritual.

Start by laying your white cloth on the table and placing your glass of water onto it. Imagining the glass of water filled with a golden light. Take a pinch of salt and slowly watch the granules fall into the water. Use your fingers to sprinkle the salty water onto your Gem-Crystal Talisman, whilst still imagining the golden light shining in the water.

Next, pass your Talisman through the smoke from the incense stick to symbolically purify it. Hold it there for a short while, and then pass your talisman through the flame of the candle, which symbolises the cleansing away of all the impurities. Your Talisman, having now been cleansed, is ready to be 'charged'.

Take your Talisman, close your eyes and hold it in your passive hand so as to receive. Start to imagine a sphere of golden light radiating from above in all directions, just like a small sun. Concentrate all your energy into this sphere and by using your imagination, start to feel its power and brilliance grow.

Imagine a beam of golden light being directed from it, and being focused onto the top of your head. Imagine it descending through your body and into the ground. Feel the heat, the warmth and the energy, just as you would feel the sudden warmth of the sun as it comes out from behind a cloud.

Now imagine a second beam of light. The colour's changed to white, and it is being directed from your solar plexus directly towards your Talisman. Start to imagine your desire or object that you are wanting to achieve. Hold the thought for a moment, and then let go; relax. Your Talisman is now fully charged and beginning to work for you, in perfect harmony with 'Universal Life'.

Be prepared for positive changes - they are about to come.

To protect yourself from any random negative energy whilst performing the above ritual, it would be wise, before you start, to 'affirm' with a prayer. Here's an example:

'I ask only the highest forces of God, my higher self or my guides and angels to work through this Talisman.
This I ask in the name of Love and for the good of all'.

As with any sincere practice of prayer, visualisation, ritual or magic, the power comes from the intention - that wise connection between the self and that which is divine, the 'Universal Life Force'.

Live the journery - the journey is Life.

See your local stockist first, for any Gemstones and Crystals mentioned in this publication. If you are having difficulty obtaining any of the stones mentioned, we do offer our own mail order service and would be more than pleased to supply any of the stones listed in the form of Tumblestones. These are smooth, rounded stones ideal for use as Birthstones or as Healing Crystals.

For further details - write to:
Rosewood
P.O. Box 219, Huddersfield, West Yorkshire. HD2 2YT

E-mail enquiries to: info@rosewood-gifts.co.uk

Or why not visit our website for even more information:

www. rosewood-gifts.co.uk

Other titles in the 'POWER FOR LIFE' series:

Discover your own Special Birthstone and the renowned Healing Powers of Crystals REF. (BK1) A look at Birthstones, personality traits and characteristics associated with each Sign of the Zodiac – plus a guide to the author's own unique range of Power Gems.

A Special Glossary of Healing Stones plus Birthstones REF. (BK2) An introduction to Crystal Healing, with an invaluable Glossary listing common ailments and suggesting combinations of Gemstones/Crystals.

Create a Wish Kit using a Candle, a Crystal and the Imagination of Your Mind REF. (BK3) 'The key to happiness is having dreams; the key to success is making dreams come true.' This book will help you achieve.

Gemstone & Crystal Elixirs – Potions for Love, Health, Wealth, Energy and Success REF. (BK4) An ancient form of 'magic', invoking super-natural powers. You won't believe the power you can get from a drink!

Crystal Pendulum for Dowsing REF. (BK5) An ancient knowledge for unlocking your Psychic Power, to seek out information not easily available by any other means. Contains easy-to-follow instructions.

Crystal Healing – Fact or Fiction? Real or Imaginary? REF. (BK6) Find the answer in this book. Discover a hidden code used by Jesus Christ for healing, and read about the science of light and colour. It's really amazing.

How to Activate the Hidden Power in Gemstones and Crystals REF. (BK7) The key is to energise the thought using a crystal. The conscious can direct – but discover the real power. It's all in this book.

Astrology: The Secret Code REF. (BK8) In church it's called 'Myers Briggs typology'. In this book it's called 'psychological profiling'. If you read your horoscope, you need to read this to find your true birthstone.

A Guide to the Mysteries surrounding Gemstones & Crystals REF. (BK10) Crystal healing, birthstones, crystal gazing, lucky talismans, elixirs, crystal dowsing, astrology, rune stones, amulets and rituals.

A Simple Guide to Gemstone & Crystal Power – a mystical A-Z of stones REF. (BK11) From Agate to Zircon, all you ever needed or wanted to know about the mystical powers of gemstones and crystals.

Change Your Life by Using the Most Powerful Crystal on Earth REF. (BK12) The most powerful crystal on earth can be yours. A book so disarmingly simple to understand, yet with a tremendous depth of knowledge.

All the above books are available from your local stockist,
or, if not, from the publisher.

NOTES

Welcome to the world of Rosewood

An extract from a 'thank- you' letter for one of my books.

"I realised just how much you really had indeed understood me and my need for direction and truly have allowed me the confidence and strength to know and believe I can achieve whatever I want in life"

If you like natural products, hand-crafted gifts including Gemstone jewellery, objects of natural beauty – the finest examples from Mother Nature, tinged with an air of Mystery – then we will not disappoint you. For those who can enjoy that feeling of connection with the esoteric nature of Gemstones and Crystals, then our 'Power for Life – Power Bracelets could be ideal for you. Each bracelet comes with its own guide explaining a way of thinking that's so powerful it will change your life and the information comes straight from the Bible. e.g. read Mark 11: 22

We regularly give inspirational talks on Crystal Power – fact or fiction? A captivating story about the world's fascination with natural gemstones and crystals and how the Placebo effect explains the healing power of gemstones and crystals – it's intriguing. And it's available on a CD

To see our full range of books, jewellery and gifts including CD's and DVD'S

Visit our web site - www.rosewood-gifts.co.uk

To see our latest videos go to 'You Tube' and type in Rosewood Gifts.